D0407865

# There Was a Place and Other Poems

## ALSO BY MYRA COHN LIVINGSTON

CELEBRATIONS

THE CHILD AS POET:
MYTH OR REALITY?

A CIRCLE OF SEASONS

COME AWAY
(*A Margaret K. McElderry Book*)

EARTH SONGS

HIGGLEDY-PIGGLEDY:
VERSES AND PICTURES
(*A Margaret K. McElderry Book*)

A LOLLYGAG OF LIMERICKS
(*A Margaret K. McElderry Book*)

MONKEY PUZZLE AND OTHER POEMS
(*A Margaret K. McElderry Book*)

NO WAY OF KNOWING:
DALLAS POEMS
(*A Margaret K. McElderry Book*)

SEA SONGS

SKY SONGS

SPACE SONGS

O SLIVER OF LIVER AND OTHER POEMS
(*A Margaret K. McElderry Book*)

A SONG I SANG TO YOU

THE WAY THINGS ARE AND OTHER POEMS
(*A Margaret K. McElderry Book*)

WORLDS I KNOW AND OTHER POEMS
(*A Margaret K. McElderry Book*)

EDITED BY MYRA COHN LIVINGSTON

CALLOOH! CALLAY!
HOLIDAY POEMS FOR YOUNG READERS
*(A Margaret K. McElderry Book)*

HOW PLEASANT TO KNOW MR. LEAR!

O FRABJOUS DAY!
POETRY FOR HOLIDAYS AND SPECIAL OCCASIONS
*(A Margaret K. McElderry Book)*

POEMS OF CHRISTMAS
*(A Margaret K. McElderry Book)*

POEMS OF LEWIS CARROLL

THESE SMALL STONES

WHY AM I GROWN SO COLD?
POEMS OF THE UNKNOWABLE
*(A Margaret K. McElderry Book)*

A LEARICAL LEXICON
*(A Margaret K. McElderry Book)*

I LIKE YOU, IF YOU LIKE ME
*(A Margaret K. McElderry Book)*

# There Was a Place and Other Poems

Myra Cohn Livingston

*Margaret K. McElderry Books*
NEW YORK

Margaret K. McElderry Books
Macmillan Publishing Company
866 Third Avenue
New York, NY 10022
Collier Macmillan Canada, Inc.

Printed in the United States of America

Designed by Barbara A. Fitzsimmons

First Edition

10 9 8 7 6 5 4 3 2 1

Library of Congress Cataloging-in-Publication Data

Livingston, Myra Cohn.
There was a place and other poems.

Summary: A collection of poems with an emphasis
on interpersonal relations, describing such situations
as family life, divorce, and remarriage.
1. Children's poetry, American. [1. American
poetry] I. Title.
PS3562.I945T47 1988 811'.54 88-12832
ISBN 0-689-50464-0

CONTENTS

## LOST DOG

When I came home
and you weren't there
I wondered,
  worried—tell me where

you went
and why you
left
alone.

I've called and called.

Why are you gone?
Why did you leave?
Where did you roam?

When will you sniff your long way home?

## OLIVE STREET

I remember
Olive Street.
Living there was really neat.

We had a stucco house
and yard.
Then Dad got sick, and it was hard

for Mom to work
and pay the rent.
One year a social worker sent

me off to camp.
When I came back
we'd moved into a sort of shack

and then a place
across the way
with nowhere green for me to play.

We've moved so much
since I was eight
I can't keep all the places straight.

When Dad gets well
won't it be neat
to live again on Olive Street?

## INTERLUDE

I like to stay with Grandmother
when the going's bad.

Mom is feeling down again;
looks so old, so sad.

Can't stay long at Grandmother's.
Have to go and see

how my mom is getting on.
Mom depends on me.

## EXCUSE

Forgot my homework.

Took my stuff
   to Dad's apartment
   Sunday.

Packed up my things
And left it there.

I move to Mom's
   on
   Monday.

## FATHER

I look for you on every street,
wondering if we'll ever meet.

In every crowd I try to see
your face. I think you'd know it's me.

I watch our corner where the bus
stops, hoping you'll come back to us.

Mom says I'd better just forget
about you. But I haven't, yet.

## CIRCLES

I am speaking of circles.

The circle we made around the table,
our hands brushing as we passed potatoes.
The circle we made in our potatoes
to pour in gravy, whorling in its round bowl.
The circle we made every evening
finding our own place at the table
with its own napkin in its own ring.

I am speaking of circles broken.

## SPIDER WEB

There,
caught in
two old trees,
round as the sun,
bigger than my head,
a spider web
in silver
glistens
high
up
catching
the glints of
the setting sun
in a glittering wheel
of shimmering
bright silver
circles
as
small
insects
flitter by
in crazy flight,
and drawn close, closer,
magnetized, I
too become
one of
them

## BIRDS KNOW

Birds know how to lift their wings,
to fold their feet
to fly

across the air
to other lands
fighting the windy sky.

Birds know how to leave the cold.

One day, so will I.

## GARAGE APARTMENT

Right on the alley
   is our place.
We have one room.
   There's not much space

but there's a park
   twelve blocks away
and I sleep on
   the rollaway.

Each week
   we go to Family Aid
to get food stamps.
   Our rent is paid.

Mom took a job
   from 3 to 9.
She does her chores
   and I do mine.

One day, I dream,
   we'll have a place
nearer the park
   with lots of space.

## THERE WAS A PLACE

There was a place
we'd always walk,
look at the sky,
have a long talk.

Sit on a bench,
drink a few Cokes,
listen to Dad
telling some jokes.

Now the sky's dark.
Can't see his face.
Can't hear the jokes.
There was a place.

## NEW DAD

You won't believe it!
He's so tall!
Yesterday
we took a ball
and practiced catching,
out at the lot,
'til it turned dark.
We just forgot
that Mom was waiting.
Then we went
and ate some pizza.
Then we spent
an hour
looking at a show.
When you meet him
then you'll know
all about
a dad who's new
and likes to have
some fun
with
you.

## INVITATION

Listen! I've a big surprise!
My new mom has light-green eyes

and my new brother, almost ten,
is really smart. He helped me when

we did our homework. They moved in
a week ago. When we begin

to settle down, she said that you
could come for dinner. When you do

you'll like them, just like Dad and me,
so come and meet my family!

## RELATIONSHIP

Okay with me.
They laugh a lot,
And I think Dad's
Almost forgot

How bad it was
Before Mom died.
We stayed together
And we tried

But things are better
Now we're three.
Since Dad's okay,
Okay with me!

## MATCH

After work
he rings our bell
and asks for Mom.
It's hard to tell

if she likes him,
but I can see
he sure likes her.
He's nice to me

So I just smile
and let him in
and maybe, soon,
love will begin.

## MOUNT ST. HELENS

Tall times
are the old times,
the Mount St. Helens times,
When she towered over lowlands,
but that's

before
she blew her top,
exploded, threw rocks and,
half-gone, shrunk into a scooped-out
sandpile.

## LONG-AGO DAYS

Here's a picture
of Mom
in the old days
when she smiled
and wore a white dress.

Here's a picture
of Dad
dressed for Sunday
and smiling
beside her.

I guess

that's what happened in all of the good days,
the old days,
the days long ago.

What spoiled the smiles?
What made it all change?
What happened?

Does anyone know?

## FAMILY

Momma and T.J. and Katie and me,
We're all we need for a family.

Used to have Poppa but he ran away.
Last time we heard from him, middle of May,

He'd gone to Montana and married again.
Mom says she's through with all runaway men.

Mom says that T.J. and Katie and me
Make the best kind of a real family.

## IN THE MIDDLE

Mom
says
she wants me

more than Dad.

How do I ever choose?

Dad
says
he wants me

more than Mom.

Somebody has to lose.

## OTHERS

Went over to Heather's.
She had a mom
Saying "Come in."
The kitchen was warm

With chicken pie cooking.
In came her dad
Who gave her a kiss.
Everyone had

Something to talk about,
Something to say.
Wish I could go to their house
Every day.

## LETTER

Come and see me. I have grown. The bicycle
I used to own is too small now. Mine's brand-
new. Please come. I'll make a sign for you
with W*E*L*C*O*M*E on it. We can play a
game of checkers every day, and watch TV, and
after that? Please come. I'll bet you miss the
cat. There are three kittens now and she will
purr at you like she does me. Please come. I
need to see your face fill up our rooms of empty
space.

## LATE AFTERNOON

Soon as I come home from school he is there,
Reading a magazine, drinking a Coke,
Waiting around while Mom does up her hair.

How's life? He smiles. How are things going?
Closes his magazine, tells me a joke,
Waiting for Mom to come. No way of knowing

How long he'll be here, how long he'll stay;
Pulls out a cigarette, has a long smoke.
House stays all smelly 'til he goes away.

## HIS GIRLFRIEND

She smiles a lot.
She's pretty, I guess.
She tries to be nice,
  but it's really a mess

  to go out and have fun,
  pretending you care,
  laughing at jokes,

  when your real mom's not there.

## MOTHER

Behind the window
I saw her there,

Standing still
With a far-off stare,

Watching the sky
And sultry air

Nothing but time
And time to spare.

No one to call her.
No one to care.

## LOVE

Wish they'd kiss each other,
hug each other tight,
laugh a lot and tell some jokes,
never have a fight.

Wish they'd say some words of love
like other people do,
look into each other's eyes.
*Wish my wish comes true!*

## JUNE: MOURNING DOVES

Where mourning-dove mother built her nest
Mourning-dove father came to rest.

She cooed to him on a nearby bough
And he to her, and then, somehow

She ruffled and moved, making a space
For him to sit, and in that place

They keep their little white eggs warm,
Hidden beneath them, safe from harm.

# HOME

Yelling,
shouting,
arguing,
their faces scrunch up tight.

Slamming doors,
clenching fists,
they battle half the night.

Cursing,
hissing,
screaming out
their hates, their rights, their wrongs—

Who am I?
What am I?
Where do I belong?

## HELP?

Would it help
  if I could say

  *Don't worry,* Mom,

  and if I pray
  when Dad comes home
  he'll want to stay?

Would it help?
  No way. No way.

## FEBRUARY 14

Who needs
  red hearts
  and paper lace?

  Love won't live in this sad old place,
  or find a kiss or happy face.

I write "I love you" and erase
  this stupid Valentine.

## THE SECRET

We don't mention where he went.
We don't say that he was sent

Somewhere, where he has to learn
How to act, then return

Back to us and get along.
We don't say he did things wrong.

We don't know if he'll be well.
We don't say it. We don't tell.

## FINDING A WAY

I'd like you for a friend.
I'd like to find the way
Of asking you to be my friend.
I don't know what to say.

What would you like to hear?
What is it I can do?
There has to be some word, some look
Connecting me to you.

## A BEGINNING

Think about the way we'll meet.
I'll be walking down the street.

Suddenly you'll see my eyes,
Look at me with such surprise.

I'll ask, "Do I know your name?"
You'll stop short and do the same.

We'll stand there and then you'll say
How you're glad we met today.

I'll leave soon and hurry home.
You'll call on the telephone

Saying "Hi, how have you been?"
That's the way we can begin.

## SEA SHELL

Sea shell,
  I will take you home
  where you will sing to me
  of waves you rode in an angry storm,
  fighting the wild sea.

And I will sing to you,
  sea shell,
  the dreams of a child tossed
  over the waves of another storm;
  both of us lone and lost.